Canada's Law on Child Sexual Abuse

A HANDBOOK

by Mary Wells, BA, BSW

Canadian Cataloguing in Publication Data

Wells, Mary

Canada's law on child sexual abuse: a handbook

Issued also in French under title: L'exploitation sexuelle des enfants et la législation
canadienne : Manuel
"Project of the Law Information Section of the Policy, Programs and Research Sector,
Department of Justice Canada."
Includes bibliographic references and an index.
"JUS-P-540E"
DSS cat. no. J2-93/1990E
ISBN 0-662-17857-2

1. Child molesting -- Law and legislation -- Canada -- Handbooks, manuals, etc.
2. Sex crimes -- Canada -- Investigation -- Handbooks, manuals, etc.
3. Social work with children -- Canada -- Handbooks, manuals, etc.
I. Canada. Dept. of Justice. II Canada. Law Information Section. III. Title

KE8926.W44 1989   345.71'02536   C90-098590-9

Published by authority of the Minister of Justice
and Attorney General of Canada

by

Communications and Public Affairs
Department of Justice Canada
Ottawa, Ontario
K1A 0H8
(613) 957-4222

Également disponible en français sous le titre **L'exploitation sexuelle des enfants et
la législation canadienne : Manuel**

This handbook has been written to provide child protection workers with information
on Canada's child sexual abuse legislation. As well, this information will be of interest
to others working in the field of child sexual abuse. The handbook is also intended to
stimulate thought and discussion on the effects of the reform of the law. It should not,
however, be viewed as a substitute for legal advice.

ABOUT THE AUTHOR

Mary Wells is a social worker who has been practising in the field of child welfare since 1970. In the early 1980s, as a social worker for Justice for Children (a community legal clinic), she began to receive referrals from child protection workers asking for assistance in preparing children to testify in child sexual abuse court cases. Through this experience, she realized that these children faced special problems and needed special assistance.

Since that time, Mary Wells has worked extensively in the field of child sexual abuse, developing methods of child witness preparation and specialized treatment approaches that address the unique dynamics of child sexual abuse. She now has a small private clinical practice and is a staff member with the Institute for the Prevention of Child Abuse in Toronto, where she leads child sexual abuse training sessions for police, and for family and child service agencies.

ACKNOWLEDGMENTS

I would like to thank the following individuals who provided consultation during the development of this handbook:

Nicholas Bala
Professor, Faculty of Law
Queen's University
Kingston, Ontario

John Pepper
Assistant Crown Attorney
Renfrew, Ontario

Marcellina Mian
Pediatrician and Director
Suspected Child Abuse and Neglect Program
Hospital for Sick Children
Toronto, Ontario

Special thanks are extended to the staff of the Legal Resource Centre, Faculty of Extension, University of Alberta, for their many hours of editorial consultation and diligent review; to Marie Gauthier, Law Information Program Officer, Department of Justice Canada, for her persistence, enthusiasm and encouragement; and to Dale MacMurray, Head, Creative Services, Communications and Public Affairs, Department of Justice Canada, for his fine editing.

Finally, I wish to express my deep gratitude to my husband and son who were endlessly supportive while "Mom wrote the book".

Mary Wells

TABLE OF CONTENTS

PREFACE

Under Canada's legal system, the federal government has authority for the criminal law and the provincial and territorial governments have responsibility for the administration of justice.

The *Criminal Code* and the *Canada Evidence Act* are two federal laws covering criminal justice matters that also have implications for the provincial and territorial administration of justice. With the coming into force of the new provisions of these laws concerning the sexual abuse of children, the provincial and territorial governments have revised their laws and are considering what other changes to provincial and territorial practices may be required to accommodate the new provisions.

As is the case with any law, the new sections of the *Criminal Code* and the *Canada Evidence Act* are the subject of careful scrutiny and interpretation by judges across Canada. The meaning of many terms used in the new law will be clarified through this process; as a result, its full impact will not be known for some time.

Canada's criminal justice system is based on a codified statement of criminal law complemented by the common law. Under this system, every case before the courts potentially contributes to the development of a body of case law, referred to as jurisprudence, containing precedents that guide future judgments. Every case, therefore, may have a part in shaping the effect of the law's provisions. It is this dynamic process that will give meaning to the new legislation that attempts to better protect children and young people from sexual abuse.

Active, diligent participation by the professionals involved in bringing the elements of each case before the court can affect its outcome. Persons involved in child sexual abuse investigations face a significant challenge, in that their work may influence early, precedent-setting decisions as cases are brought forward under the new law. This handbook has been written so that a clear understanding of the new law will create a foundation for standards of practice.

INTRODUCTION

Using this Handbook

The changes to the *Criminal Code* and the *Canada Evidence Act* on January 1, 1988, created new child sexual abuse offences and expanded the opportunities for courts to receive children's testimony in cases of child sexual abuse.

This has major implications for professionals working with sexually abused children. Social workers, in particular when they are acting as child protection workers,* will find themselves increasingly participating in investigative activities and may be required to give evidence at criminal trials.

Information about the new law and its implications for social work practice is essential background, especially with regard to child sexual abuse investigations. The new law also creates a special need for close cooperation between the criminal justice system and the child welfare system.

who will find this handbook of interest?

This handbook is written primarily for social workers acting as child protection workers, but is expected to be of interest to the social-work profession generally. It may also be of use to other professionals such as police officers, lawyers, school personnel, child-care workers, mental health clinicians, victim advocates, public health nurses and physicians. People working with children may want to read the handbook in order to

---

* For the purposes of this handbook, a child protection worker is an employee of a social service agency, an officially designated service or a Children's Aid Society, responsible for providing services to abused children.

understand some of the issues with which child protection workers deal in attempting to respond to and protect sexually abused children. In addition, members of the general public who are seeking greater insight into the law on child sexual abuse and how it may be applied may find the handbook of interest.

what is this handbook about?

The handbook:

- outlines the criminal justice process and its principles

- explains the law on child sexual abuse and some of the implications it may hold for investigative practices and management of evidence

- discusses the need for the adaptation of investigative methods when a child sexual abuse case becomes a criminal justice matter

- explains changes in the rules of evidence relating to child witnesses, particularly the rules that have been designed to offset the disadvantages previously experienced by child witnesses, and

- suggests roles child protection workers may assume under the new law.

how this handbook can be used

- The handbook can be used to understand the specific changes brought about by the January 1, 1988, amendments to the *Criminal Code* and the *Canada Evidence Act* dealing with child sexual abuse.

- It can be used as a guide to the steps that can be followed when interviewing and preparing children for court.

- It can be consulted as a reference manual on the new law.

- It can be read in its entirety for a general understanding of what the Canadian criminal justice system's approach will now be in responding to child victims of sexual abuse.

Each chapter of the handbook provides a discussion of some of the implications of various aspects of the new law for social-work practice. In some chapters, discussions are expanded by question-and-answer sections. Examples are provided to help the reader understand general principles and concepts **but they are not intended to provide legal opinions and are not to be relied on in similar situations.**

Child Sexual Abuse: Historical Perspectives

Recognition of, and concern about, the problem of child sexual abuse has grown over the centuries. Florence Rush, in her book, *The Best Kept Secrets*,[1] traces the history of the law regarding child sexual abuse. In England, the crime of child rape was not separated from church law until the thirteenth century, when it became a misdemeanour (not a felony) for a man to ravish a female under the age of twelve, even if she did not resist. In 1571, public confusion about child rape became apparent when "one W.D." was acquitted of raping a seven-year-old, despite the evidence of eye-witnesses, because the jurists "doubted a rape in so tender a child". In other words, it just could not have happened.

The sexual abuse of children did not appear to be a major cause of concern until the late nineteenth century. At that time, public attention was focused not so much on the plight of

---

[1] Florence Rush, *The Best Kept Secrets: Sexual Abuse of Children*, McGraw-Hill, New York, 1980.

sexually abused children but on widespread anxiety over an outbreak of venereal disease related to flourishing prostitution. One study showed that of 2,582 women arrested in Paris for prostitution, 1,500 were minors. An 1899 conference on prostitution drew experts who agreed that close to 70 per cent of all prostitutes suffered from syphilis before the age of twenty-one. "Deflowered at sixteen, prostitute at seventeen, syphilitic at eighteen" became a common observation.

About the same time, Freud, who initially was convinced that many of his hysterical patients were suffering from the trauma of childhood seduction, abandoned this belief out of personal conflict and under pressure from colleagues. His seduction theory turned into the "seduction fantasy", leading to generations of therapists who held suspect the statements of women and children who described childhood sexual abuse.

This belief in the tendency of women and children to fabricate stories of abuse entered into the body of legal theory, causing a reluctance to prosecute these cases. In 1934 John Henry Wigmore enshrined this notion in legal theory when he cautioned against sexual assault prosecutions. He said that women and children are predisposed to bring false accusations against men of good character and should be psychiatrically examined before being allowed to testify.[2]

Resistance to the idea of child sexual abuse permeated public attitudes until the mid-twentieth century, when writers such as Rush and others began to clamour for a reevaluation of this thinking.

---

[2] John Henry Wigmore, *Evidence in Trials at Common Law,* Little, Brown and Company, Toronto, 1970. Volume 3A.

Canada's response

In Canada, sexual offences against children and youth began to be recognized as a serious problem in the late 1970s. In December 1980, Parliament established a special committee to enquire fully into the matter and make recommendations. The Report of the Committee on Sexual Offences Against Children and Youth (the Badgley Report) confirmed what front-line personnel were beginning to suspect: child sexual abuse is a problem of major proportions, having significant implications for Canada's children.

The Committee's recommendations included a strong emphasis on the need to invoke criminal sanctions for offenders, both for deterrence and for rehabilitation purposes. The Committee clearly described child sexual abuse as a criminal behaviour, not a simple, non-victimizing mental health problem.

child sexual abuse: its nature and extent

The Committee found that:

- At some time during their lives, about one in two females and one in three males had been victims of one or more unwanted sexual acts. These acts included witnessing an indecent exposure, being touched on a sexual part of the body, being sexually threatened, and being subject to an attempted or an actual sexual assault.

- About four in five of these unwanted sexual acts had first been committed against these persons when they were children or youths.

- Four in one hundred young females had been raped.

- Two in one hundred young persons had experienced attempted or actual acts of unwanted anal penetration by a penis, or by means of objects or fingers.

- Acts of exposure constituted the largest single category of sexual offences committed against children. Cases were documented where such acts were followed by sexual assault.

- Three in five sexually abused children had been threatened or physically coerced by their assailants. Young victims were as likely to be threatened or forced to engage in sexual acts by persons relatively close to their age as by older persons.

- Although few young victims were physically injured, substantially more suffered emotional harm.

- About one in four assailants was a family member or a person in a position of trust, about half were friends or acquaintances, and about one in six was a stranger.

- Nearly all assailants were males; one in one hundred was a female.

- A majority of the victims or their families did not seek assistance from public services. When they did, they turned most often to police and doctors.

- Although child sexual abuse was not typically characterized by violence, in those instances where violence occurred, it was very serious. More than two in five of all sexual assault homicides were committed against children aged 15 and younger.[3]

---

[3] *Sexual Offences Against Children*, Ottawa, Supply and Services Canada, 1984. Two volumes, 1,314 pages.

At about the same time that the Badgley Report emerged, child sexual abuse began to be reported and verified with much higher frequency by child protection agencies across the country. This upward swing in reporting sexual abuse put child protection workers squarely on the line in cases that contained criminal justice implications.

The federal government moved to implement the recommendations of the Badgley Report, and in January 1988 a major reform to the criminal law was proclaimed, making it easier to prosecute child sexual abusers.

The law, while paying attention to the concern that accused persons should not be deprived of fundamental rights to a fair trial, creates a series of new offences and defences, and increases the opportunities for children to testify in court. It is anticipated that the law will help to increase the number of successful prosecutions.

Chapter 1

Highlights
of Canada's Law
on Child
Sexual Abuse

Why a Change in the Criminal Law?

Although provincial or territorial child protection laws can be used to place children under protective supervision or to remove them from abusive situations, these laws have limitations. They are not designed to actively prevent people from engaging in abusive behaviour. As well, courts handling child welfare matters have no power to convict people of criminal acts or to pass sentences in order to deter such acts.

The Badgley Report documented the limited ability of the pre-1988 federal law to protect children from the recurrence of sexual abuse. Research referred to in the report indicated that the *Criminal Code* definitions of sexual offences against children were inadequate to deal with the sexual abuse of children. In addition, laws on the rules of evidence and the rules of procedure required that a child's testimony always be supported by other testimony. These rules usually did not provide younger children with the chance to testify. As a result, it was often difficult to call in the powers of the criminal justice system to deal with incidents of child sexual abuse. As victims, children therefore did not enjoy the same protection that adults had before the law.

In recognition of these "gaps" in the law, Bill C-15 was introduced in Parliament and amendments were made to the *Criminal Code* and the *Canada Evidence Act*. The changes came into effect on January 1, 1988.

Sexual Offences Against Children

There are now 16 sexual offences in the *Criminal Code* that could apply to child sexual abuse:

Sexual interference
Invitation to sexual touching
Sexual exploitation of a young person
Anal intercourse
Bestiality
Parent or guardian procuring sexual activity of a child
Householder permitting sexual activity
Exposing genitals to a child
Vagrancy
Offences in relation to juvenile prostitution
    a) Living off the avails of child prostitution
    b) Attempting to obtain the sexual services of a child
Incest
Corrupting children
Indecent acts
Sexual assault
Sexual assault with a weapon, threats to a third party or causing bodily harm
Aggravated sexual assault

These offences are discussed in detail in Chapter 3.

Other Elements of the Law

consent

- Sexual activity **without consent** is always a crime regardless of the age of the individuals.

- The definitions of the crimes in the new law reinforce the fact that children need to be protected. Individuals who sexually abuse children are not able to avoid criminal responsibility by claiming a child "consented" to the abuse.

- Children under 12 are never considered able to consent to sexual activity.

- Children 12 or more, but under 14, are deemed unable to consent to sexual acts except under specific circumstances involving sexual activity with their peers.

- Young persons 14 or more but under 18 are protected from sexual exploitation and their consent is not valid if the person touching them for a sexual purpose is in a position of trust or authority over them or if they are in a relationship of dependency with that person.

- It is not a defence to these crimes for the accused to say that he or she believed the young person was older. The person accused of the crime has to prove that all "reasonable steps", such as asking for identification showing proof of age, were taken.

sexual activity between young people

- It is recognized that adolescents, as part of their normal development, may engage in some sexual exploration. To allow for this, the law says that it is not a crime for two adolescents who are close to the same age to agree to sexual activity. The consent of both adolescents is, of course, essential.

- In cases where the alleged victim is 12 or more but under 14, the defence that the victim consented to the sexual activity can therefore be raised by an adolescent accused of sexual abuse. This defence can be accepted by the court if the accused is less than two years older than the victim and is not yet 16 years of age. However, the defence is not available if the accused is in a position of trust or authority in relation to the victim or if the victim is in a relationship of dependency with the accused.

- The age of consent for anal intercourse taking place in private between consenting individuals is 18, unless the young persons are married to each other.

Rules Regarding Child Witnesses

The rules of evidence have also been changed to make it easier for children's evidence of sexual abuse to be heard in court.

- In prosecutions of child sexual abuse, corroboration (supporting evidence) of a child victim's or witness's testimony is no longer required to convict an accused.

- As in the 1983 changes to the *Criminal Code* concerning adult sexual assault cases, the former rule on "recent complaint" has been removed from all child sexual abuse cases. This rule required the court to hold in doubt the testimony of a sexual abuse victim who did not complain to someone immediately after the offence occurred.

- With certain exceptions, evidence may not be introduced concerning the victim's sexual activity with any person other than the accused.

- With respect to the new offences, evidence of the victim's reputation is not admissible for the purposes of supporting or challenging the credibility of the child victim or witness.

- The court must make an order prohibiting the publication or broadcasting of information that would identify the child victim or any witness under 18, if asked to do so by the crown prosecutor, the victim or the witness.

- Children may testify even if the court finds that they are not able to understand the nature of an oath or solemn affirmation. To testify, however, they must be able to "communicate the evidence" and have to promise to tell the truth.

- Child victims may testify from behind a screen or other device within the courtroom or in an out-of-courtroom setting via closed-circuit television. This is allowed where the judge is of the opinion that these measures are necessary and where there is evidence that testifying in front of the accused would prevent the child victim from giving a full and candid account of the sexual offence.

but

When a child victim testifies outside the courtroom, the accused, the judge, and jury, if there is one, must be allowed to observe the giving of all testimony. The accused must be able to communicate with his or her lawyer at all times.

- Videotaped statements made by the child victim about the sexual abuse, if recorded within a "reasonable time" after the incident, will be admissible if the child, as a witness in court, adopts the contents of the videotape.

- The defence lawyer or the accused continues to have the right to cross-examine the child victim and all other witnesses testifying for the prosecution.

Review Process

In recognition of the fact that only implementation of the new law will yield a clear picture of its ramifications, strengths and weaknesses, a review process has been established. According to the law, Parliament must, in 1992, ask a committee of Parliament to review the provisions of the child sexual abuse legislation and to present a report as soon as possible.

Chapter 2

The Criminal Justice Process at a Glance

Combining the Child Protection and Criminal Justice Functions

When a child has been sexually abused, there exists a societal responsibility not only to ensure the ongoing protection of the child, but also to prevent the abuser from continuing with any further abusive behaviour toward this child or any other child. Child abusers must be held accountable for their actions.

The child welfare system is in place to protect children, while the criminal justice system protects society from harmful acts and sets forth consequences for offenders. As the criminal justice system and the child welfare system carry out these dual responsibilities, their paths necessarily meet and cross. Increasingly, police forces, crown prosecutors and child protection agencies are developing collaborative, teamwork approaches in responding to child sexual abuse.

Because each system has a different mandate, short-term objectives may differ, but both ultimately have the same goal of protecting society's members. With a mandate to protect children, the guiding principles of the child welfare system include respect for the integrity of the individual, support for the family and the use of the least intrusive measures necessary to ensure the safety of the child. The criminal justice system, on the other hand, is dedicated to the maintenance of law and order.

Although both the child welfare system and the criminal justice system strive to protect individuals, they must also preserve individual liberty and maintain minimum interference by the state into people's private lives.

Protecting Children and Society While Safeguarding Individual Freedoms

Before looking at the new law on child sexual abuse, it is useful to review the general principles of the Canadian system of justice. Prosecutions of cases of child sexual abuse are governed by a set of rules that are designed not only to protect victims, but also to protect the rights of the accused. If this did not happen – if the rights of accused persons were not protected – the law would only be "protecting" our children to grow up in a society where their own right to freedom would be tenuous at best.

The fundamental principles of the Canadian justice system are stated in the *Canadian Charter of Rights and Freedoms* and are also found in the *Criminal Code* and in case law.

The most important rule in Canadian criminal law is that a person is presumed innocent until proven guilty in court.

Safeguards are in place to ensure that people accused of a crime are treated fairly and are given the maximum opportunity to prove their innocence.

- People who are charged with committing an offence have the right to be told the precise nature of the accusation.

- They have the possibility of remaining free while awaiting trial. If they are held in custody and then released, they must receive a written release that explains any conditions that may have been set and specifies when they must appear in court.

- They have the right to have their guilt or innocence determined by a judge, or in some cases by a judge and jury, in an open court following a full and fair trial.

- They have the right to hear evidence against them in open court.

- They have the right to challenge, in cross-examination, the evidence presented by the prosecution, and to present their own evidence.

- They have the right to remain silent at the trial. An accused does not have to testify at his or her trial and the fact that the accused did not testify at the trial cannot be used as evidence of guilt.

While the criminal justice process has as its goal the protection of society, it is of equal concern that criminal justice be pursued with the greatest of care by ensuring that individuals are not unfairly deprived of their liberty. These safeguards exist in order to eliminate the risk of an innocent person being convicted. However, the rights of the accused are balanced with society's need to protect all its citizens. Courts must sometimes make decisions that deprive some people of a fundamental freedom in order to protect others.

Proving Guilt at a Trial

A person accused of a crime will not be found guilty unless the court is convinced that:

- a crime occurred;

- the accused is the person who committed the crime; and

- he or she intended to commit the crime.

Where there is an allegation that a criminal act has occurred and a person is charged, the charge must state the specific offence or offences under the *Criminal Code*.

The effects of a finding of criminal guilt can be very serious, including the deprivation of fundamental liberties. That is why the standard of proof in criminal law is a high one and an accused person is presumed to be innocent until proven guilty **beyond a reasonable doubt**. This is in contrast to the standard of proof required to prove that a child is "in need of protection" under provincial or territorial laws. For this finding to be made, the court need only be convinced **on the balance of probabilities** that the child is in need of protection.

Because of the different standards of proof, it sometimes happens that a provincial or territorial family court holding a hearing under child welfare legislation will make a finding that a child is "in need of protection" and may issue an order to protect the child, even though the person accused of abusing the child is acquitted of criminal charges.

CANADIAN CRIMINAL COURT STRUCTURE

Supreme Court of Canada

Court of Appeal
Appellate Division of Provincial Superior Court

Provincial Superior Court

County or District Court *

Provincial/Territorial Court **

* There are county or district courts in only three provinces: Nova Scotia, Ontario and British Columbia.

** In Quebec, the provincial court is now known as the Court of Quebec, which includes three divisions: civil, criminal and penal, and youth.

Criminal Justice System Procedure

the criminal court structure

When looking at the criminal justice system, it is important to keep in mind that although the federal government is responsible for determining the content of the criminal law, the provinces are generally responsible for the administration of justice, including the creation and the maintenance of courts, and for law enforcement. With respect to the Yukon and the Northwest Territories, the federal government retains responsibility for prosecutions and law enforcement of territorial statutes and all federal statutes (including the *Criminal Code*).

Although the names of the courts are not the same in each province, the court system is basically the same across Canada. Generally, the courts deal with both "civil" and "criminal" matters. The court that hears a case is usually determined by the nature of the matter.

In most provinces, there are two levels of courts. However, in Nova Scotia, Quebec, Ontario and British Columbia, there are three levels. The first level is the provincial or territorial court, which deals with most criminal offences. (In Quebec, this court is called the Court of Quebec.) This level may also include certain specialized courts such as youth and family courts. Judges at this level are appointed by the provincial governments.

Nova Scotia, Ontario and British Columbia have an intermediate level of courts, called the county or district courts. The judges in these courts are appointed by the federal government. They deal with some criminal matters, hear summary conviction appeals from the provincial court, and handle civil cases.

At the highest level in a province is the superior court. An appellate division of this court or a separate court of appeal also hears appeals from all other courts in both civil and criminal matters. Judges in these courts are also appointed by the federal government. They deal with the most serious civil and criminal cases and have authority to grant divorces.

The Supreme Court of Canada is the highest court in Canada. It hears appeals from decisions of the courts of appeal. This court is usually called upon to decide important questions of interpretation concerning the Constitution and controversial areas of civil and criminal law. Its judgment in a case is final. There is no appeal from a Supreme Court decision.

types of criminal offences

The *Criminal Code* divides offences into two categories: summary conviction offences and indictable offences.

Summary conviction offences are generally less serious offences that are tried in a provincial or territorial court, before a judge only. Unless the *Criminal Code* sets out a specific penalty for the summary conviction offence, the maximum penalty is a $2,000 fine or six months in jail, or both. Summary conviction charges must be laid within six months of the offence.

Indictable offences are more serious crimes and carry the possibility of more serious sentences (up to life imprisonment). They are generally tried in a lengthier process that offers more options for the accused. For most of these offences, the accused may choose to be tried by a judge sitting alone, or by a judge sitting with a jury. If the accused chooses to be tried by a district or superior court judge sitting alone or by a judge sitting with a jury, a preliminary inquiry will be held to determine if there is enough evidence to justify committing the accused to trial. The accused may, with the consent of the Crown, waive the right to have a preliminary inquiry and go directly to the trial stage.

The *Criminal Code* specifies whether an offence is a summary conviction offence or an indictable offence. With respect to certain offences, the Code says that the offence can be prosecuted either by summary conviction or by indictment. These offences are called **dual or hybrid offences.** In these cases, the crown prosecutor, in consultation with the police, has the option of deciding to proceed by way of summary conviction or by indictment.

Categories of Child Sexual Abuse Offences

Summary Conviction
- exposing genitals to a child
- vagrancy
- indecent acts

Hybrid
- sexual interference
- invitation to sexual touching
- sexual exploitation of a young person
- anal intercourse
- bestiality
- sexual assault

Indictable
- parents or guardian procuring sexual activity of a child
- owner, manager, or occupier of premises permitting a child to engage in illegal sexual activity
- living off the avails of child prostitution
- attempting to obtain the sexual services of a child
- incest
- corrupting children
- sexual assault with a weapon, threats to a third party or causing bodily harm
- aggravated sexual assault

investigating a complaint

When an incident of child sexual abuse is reported to the police, they will conduct an investigation. The specific procedures followed in an investigation are determined by local, provincial or territorial practices. In general, the criminal investigation is done in cooperation with child protection personnel conducting a simultaneous child protection investigation. Information arising out of the investigation by police may justify the laying of charges against a suspect. In most jurisdictions in Canada, a basic element of these parallel investigations is that the police make the first contact with the accused.

arrest and release

When the police determine that a child sexual abuse crime has been committed and believe they have identified the person who committed it, a number of options are available, depending on the circumstances.

They can decide not to arrest the suspect but to tell him or her that a charge will be laid and that a summons to go to court on a specific day will be given to the person later.

Or, the police can issue an appearance notice, a written notice of the charge that specifies when the person has to go to court.

Or, the police can sometimes arrest the person and take him or her to the police station. The police must inform the person of the reason for their arrest and their right to consult a lawyer. In many cases, the senior police officer in charge can release the person if he or she promises to appear in court on a specific date, and to observe the conditions regarding his or her release.

In some cases, the person will be arrested and kept in custody. A bail hearing must be held as soon as possible. At this hearing, a justice of the peace or a judge will decide if there are circumstances to justify keeping the accused in custody until the trial. A person will be kept in custody only if the court is concerned that he or she will not return to court, or that the public interest cannot otherwise be protected. Usually, an accused will be released on promising to appear in court when required.

Conditions also can be set on the terms of the release. For instance, the accused can be ordered not to communicate with the child victim or with any of the witnesses, or not to leave the city or province. Breaking these conditions may be grounds to review the terms of the release and to set new ones, to revoke the accused's release and to order that the accused be held in custody until the trial, or may even involve an additional charge. Revoking the release or changing the restrictions is not automatic; the court must be convinced that the changes are necessary to ensure that the accused will return to court or for the public's protection.

summary conviction offence procedure

All people charged with committing sexual offences against children must go to a provincial court (territorial court or Court of Quebec) for their first court appearance. If the offence is a summary conviction matter, the court will be informed of the nature of the charge or charges and the accused will be asked for a plea of guilty or not guilty. If the accused pleads not guilty, the court judge will set aside a trial date. It could be several months before the trial begins. All summary conviction matters are heard by a provincial court judge sitting alone. There is never a jury.

indictable offence procedure

If an accused person is charged with an indictable offence (or a hybrid offence that the crown prosecutor has decided to deal with as an indictable matter), the trial process could be different. At the first court appearance the exact charges will be read.

Unless the offence is under the absolute jurisdiction of a provincial court judge, the judge does not ask for a plea, but rather asks the accused by which court he or she has decided to be tried. The accused can choose to be tried by a judge of the provincial court. In that case, the accused will be asked for a plea and the process will be the same as for a summary conviction offence. Or, the accused can decide to be tried in a superior court by a judge sitting alone or by a judge sitting with a jury. In that case, the accused is entitled to a preliminary inquiry.

It may be several months after the accused's first court appearance before a preliminary inquiry occurs. The child victim and several other witnesses will probably have to give evidence at this hearing. On rare occasions, the accused may decide to call witnesses on his or her behalf. The preliminary inquiry is not a full trial but a hearing held to determine if there is enough evidence to justify a trial. If a judge decides that there is not enough evidence to justify a trial, charges against the accused will be dropped.

The date for the trial cannot be set until after the preliminary inquiry is held, and it may be several months before the trial takes place in a higher court. Adjournments sometimes occur, often as a result of scheduling problems, and these can also delay the process.

Whether or not the accused will be kept in custody pending the trial will depend on the same considerations that apply in the summary conviction process.

the trial

When the trial takes place, the crown prosecutor will call upon the child victim and other witnesses to present the facts of the case to the court. After each witness testifies about his or her knowledge of the incident, the defence lawyer or the accused is allowed to ask questions to obtain further clarification or to challenge the evidence presented or the credibility of the witness.

This is the cross-examination. There are rules about the types of questions that may be asked to ensure that the accused's right to a fair trial is respected.

After the crown prosecutor has presented the case, the defence lawyer or the accused can call witnesses and present evidence in his or her defence. An accused is under no obligation to testify at the trial.

To convict the accused, the court must be convinced "beyond a reasonable doubt" that the evidence shows that the accused committed the crime as described in the *Criminal Code*. If there is a reasonable doubt that the accused committed the offence, the judge or the jury, in cases where there is one, must acquit the accused.

sentencing

If a finding of guilt is made by the judge or the jury, or if the accused pleads guilty, the judge must decide what punishment will be imposed. The court is limited by the maximum penalties set out for the offence in the *Criminal Code*. However, the judge has the discretion within those limits to impose a sentence that will take into account the particular circumstances of the crime and the offender. The judge is guided by principles of sentencing that have evolved through previous court decisions. Sentences given in child sexual abuse cases will be determined using the same principles of sentencing that apply to other types of offences.

Various considerations affect the formulation of the sentence. In addition to such objectives as prevention of further harm to the victim and to society, and deterrence (both with regard to the convicted person and as a general deterrent to others), reformation or rehabilitation of the convicted person is sought. Some factors will outweigh others, depending on the situation.

Mr. Justice McLennan of the Ontario Court of Appeal wrote about some of the considerations on sentencing when the Court dealt with the case of the *Queen v. Wilmott*,[4] in which a person convicted of rape appealed the length of the sentence:

> "(the sentence) . . . will depend on the nature and gravity of the crime. There should be a 'just proportion' between the crime and the sentence . . . . Other factors to be considered are whether the crime was planned or impulsive, the presence or absence of mitigating circumstances, the offender's age, his previous criminal record or absence thereof, his work record, the presence or absence of a particular crime in the community and even the offender's attitude during trial . . . this is not an exhaustive list."

The law gives a judge a great deal of choice in deciding the most appropriate punishment for each case. Although the judge can decide on the punishment from a wide range of options, the maximum possible sentence depends on the crime. Before sentencing an offender the judge may ask for a pre-sentence report, which usually is prepared by a probation officer.

Using the maximum sentence as a guide, a judge can decide on the length of the prison sentence. The maximum sentence for the new child sexual abuse crimes (invitation to sexual touching, touching for a sexual purpose and sexual exploitation) is 10 years in prison. The maximum sentence for aggravated sexual assault is life imprisonment.

The judge can also fine the offender, or order a period of probation and require that the offender report to a probation officer regularly. Other conditions of a probation order can include participating in treatment, performing community service work or not associating with certain people (for example, the child victim). If the person breaks the conditions, he or she is

---

[4] [1967] 1 C.C.C. 171

considered to have broken or "breached" the order. Breach of a probation order is itself a criminal offence.

It also should be noted that an offender can be convicted of a crime and given a conditional discharge instead of a prison term or other punishment. The lightest sentence is an absolute discharge, in which case no conviction is registered and the person is free to go.

It is possible that a child protection worker may be involved in initiating a referral to a community agency for clinical treatment of the accused. If so, this information should be made available to the Crown and the defence lawyer, who may wish to present this to the court for consideration when sentencing. The judge may accept or reject any recommendations when deciding the sentence.

In many jurisdictions, probation officers develop pre-sentence reports. Child protection case-planning documents may contain information that should be included in this report. The pre-sentence report may be used by the judge at the sentencing hearing.

After sentencing, the probation officer has responsibility for ensuring that if there are conditions of probation (such as attendance at a treatment program), they be kept. There is a clear need for good communication between the probation office and the child protection agency.

parole

If an offender is sentenced to prison, the length of the prison term is always specified in the sentence. After serving at least one third of the sentence, an offender can ask for parole. Parole is the conditional release of an offender before the full prison term has been served. It is a way of allowing a controlled and supervised return of an offender to society.

The Parole Board decides if an offender should be released before the end of the sentence, and can set conditions on the release. These can include not having any contact with children, not loitering in places that children frequent – such as parks, school grounds, recreation centres – living in a halfway house, and reporting to a parole officer on a regular basis.

When an offender is on parole, he or she has not yet completed the sentence, and a violation of the parole conditions can mean a return to prison.

Young Offenders and Child Sexual Abuse

When a young person commits a sexual offence against a child or another young person, special considerations arise. Without minimizing the nature of the offence, attention also needs to be directed to the question of whether the young person is also a victim of child sexual abuse. Is the sexually abusive behaviour a symptom of abuse? If the young person has been sexually abused, there will be a need to investigate this situation as well.

Young persons who are suspected of having committed sexual crimes against children can be charged with an offence as described in the *Criminal Code*, but they will be dealt with under the provisions of the *Young Offenders Act*. This law applies to young persons who commit crimes, and defines a "young person" as someone 12 years of age or more but who has not yet turned 18. (It should be noted that this definition of a "young person" is different from the definition in the *Criminal Code* concerning the crime of sexual exploitation. Under the Code, a "young person" is someone 14 years of age or more but who has not yet turned 18.)

The *Young Offenders Act* guarantees young people the same rights and freedoms as adults and holds them responsible for their actions. The Act, however, also recognizes that although young offenders must be held accountable for illegal behaviour, their age and degree of maturity require that they be treated differently from adults.

Young persons charged with sexual offences are dealt with in youth court. (An exception is made for youths over the age of 14 who, in serious cases such as murder charges, can be transferred to adult court for trial.) The Act also makes it possible, depending on the crime and the circumstances, to have less serious offences dealt with outside the court through a variety of alternative measures programs. These allow the young person to make amends through community service work, compensation to the victim of the crime and so on.

Sentencing in youth court is different from that in adult court, and has a strong focus on rehabilitation. The provisions of the *Young Offenders Act* allow for a full assessment of the young person before the court decides on the appropriate punishment, and are specifically designed to link sentencing with treatment.

Given the principles of the Act, which recognize the special needs of young persons, a variety of punishments are available. More likely, a young offender found guilty of a child sexual abuse crime will be put on probation, or be committed to open custody (e.g., a group home) or secure custody (e.g., a detention centre for young persons).

Careful diagnosis and the development of appropriate treatment plans are considered essential in responding to the problem of the young sexual offender. Overall, the use of the provisions of the *Young Offenders Act* may be vital in breaking the cycle of abuse while the young person's difficulties are at an early stage, and in preventing future incidents of sexual abuse.

Implications of the Criminal Justice Process for the Victim

The police and the Crown are responsible for the laying of the charges. The crown prosecutor is responsible for the presentation of the evidence of the offence at the preliminary inquiry and at the trial. The child victim is a key witness who gives evidence of the offence to the court.

The law allows child victims and child witnesses to request that their names or information that would identify them not be published or broadcast by the media. When a non-publication order is requested by a victim or a witness under 18 in a child sexual abuse case the court is required to make the order. In a situation where the accused is a young person, the publication ban is automatic.

In general, the victim does not attend the first court appearance but usually gives evidence at the preliminary inquiry and the trial. The victim will receive an official notice, a subpoena, to appear at the court hearings. It is usually up to people working closely with the victim (e.g., police, social workers, victim assistance workers, witness support workers) to keep abreast of changes such as a new trial date or new conditions of release for the accused. These workers should try to keep the victim, and the victim's parent(s) or guardian informed of developments in the case.

This can be especially important if, for example, an accused is successful in having a condition of release prohibiting contact with the victim changed. If the no-contact order is lifted and the accused returns home to live with the child victim, it may be necessary, from a child welfare perspective, to take steps to remove the child from the home.

Support for a child victim before a trial and during appearances to give evidence may be essential to ensure that the child remains emotionally able to testify. Special conditions have now been created expanding the opportunities for child victims and witnesses to testify in cases relating to child sexual abuse. These are discussed in Chapter 4.

With the proclamation of new sections of the *Criminal Code* (Bill C-89) on October 1, 1988, victims have a right to make a victim impact statement. This statement is a written and signed document given to the court before sentencing. Its purpose is to provide the judge with more information about the effect the crime has had on the victim. The police or the crown prosecutor's office can provide more information about the form of victim impact statements in a particular province or territory.

Questions and Answers

Q : Is the crown prosecutor the child victim's lawyer?

A : No. The Crown has the responsibility for presenting all the evidence of the offence to the court. In this role, the crown prosecutor represents society. He or she must strive to ensure that all the evidence is heard and that witnesses are able to give a full and candid account of their knowledge of the facts of the offence. The crown prosecutor may work closely with witnesses to this end, but it is a mistake for victims to believe that the crown prosecutor is their lawyer.

Q : Should child victims have their own lawyers?

A : Although lawyers for victims play no active role in criminal court, the family or guardian of the child may decide to retain a lawyer to attend criminal proceedings in order to obtain information for use in future civil claims against the accused for compensation for damages, cost of treatment services or other losses.

Q : Is social worker - client confidentiality protected in cases of child sexual abuse?

A : No. Social workers (and others) have a responsibility to report incidents of suspected child sexual abuse, as well as additional information about already-reported incidents, that come to their attention. It may be important to inform clients early on in the therapeutic counselling process that, in criminal proceedings involving child sexual abuse, the general rule of confidentiality does not apply.

Q : What happens when a child sexual abuse disclosure is made to a social worker or other professional?

A : A social worker or other professional should tell the client that there is a legal obligation to report the disclosure to the police or child protection agency immediately. The person being interviewed should know that the information being given will be reported.

The social worker or other professional should make careful notes of the statement and the circumstances under which it was made, since this information may be requested by the courts as evidence in the child sexual abuse matter.

However, depending on the situation, it may not be therapeutic to end the interview. The social worker should be prepared to listen and to offer support and other resources as needed.

Chapter 3

Child Sexual Abuse: A Criminal Act

Introduction

Before the amendments to the *Criminal Code* were proclaimed in January 1988, a number of criminal offences could apply if a child or young person was the victim of a sexual assault. Although the 1988 amendments created a number of new offences, some of the offences under the previous law were retained – for example, the offence of incest – and are still in force.

This chapter explains in detail both the new and the previously existing offences relating to child sexual abuse. There is a general description of each, giving the specific elements of the offence, the maximum penalty and the *Criminal Code* section reference. Some of the defences available to persons accused of committing acts of sexual abuse are also described. There is also a short discussion of each offence, including historical aspects and potential considerations for child protection workers.

It should be noted that any legislation sets limits on personal freedoms and may be subject of a court challenge under the *Canadian Charter of Rights and Freedoms*. Challenges of these new provisions of the *Criminal Code* can be expected, and the constitutionality of some of the amendments may be decided by the various courts across Canada and ultimately by the Supreme Court of Canada.

The New Offences Related to Child Sexual Abuse

Section 151 - **Sexual Interference**

Elements: Anyone who

- for a sexual purpose
- touches directly or indirectly
- with a part of the body or an object
- any part of the body
- of a child under 14.

Exception: A young person under 14 cannot be convicted of this offence, unless the young person is in a position of trust or authority in relation to the child (e.g., babysitter or parent), or is in a situation where the child victim is dependent on the young person.

Penalty: Hybrid offence –

either a)   summary – maximum penalty is a $2,000 fine or six months in jail, or both

or   b)   indictable – maximum penalty is 10 years in prison.

Discussion:

- Touching could be direct or indirect. For example, it is not a defence that the touching was done with some kind of object.

- When conducting investigative interviews with children where there has been an allegation of sexual abuse, it may be helpful to obtain information about the behaviour of the alleged offender that might indicate sexual intent. For example, did the behaviour appear to be sexually oriented (e.g. was the child's discomfort ignored and the touching geared to meet the sexual needs of the adult?)

Section 152 - **Invitation to Sexual Touching**

Elements: Every person who

- for a sexual purpose
- invites, counsels or incites
- a child under 14
- to touch directly or indirectly with a part of the body or an object
- the body of any person, including the child's own body and the body of the person encouraging the touching.

Exceptions: A young person under 14 cannot be convicted of this offence, unless the young person is in a position of trust or authority in relation to the child (e.g., a babysitter or parent), or is in a situation where the child victim is dependent on the young person.

Penalty: Hybrid offence –

either a)   summary – maximum penalty is a $2,000 fine or six months in jail, or both

or   b)   indictable – maximum penalty is 10 years in prison.

Discussion:

- This section makes it an offence for a person to invite or urge a child under the age of 14 to touch in a sexual way.

- No touching between persons has to take place for this offence to occur. For example, a person who encourages a child to masturbate commits the offence.

- In investigating complaints of sexual activity amongst a group of children, child protection workers may wish to ask questions about the presence of an older person who might have instigated the activity and who might thus be subject to prosecution.

Section 153 - **Sexual Exploitation of a Young Person**

Elements: "Young person" is defined in this section as a child 14 years of age or more but under 18.
Every person in a position of authority or trust towards a child or on whom the young person is dependent who

- for a sexual purpose
- touches a young person's body, or
- invites, counsels or incites the young person
- to touch directly or indirectly with a part of the body or an object
- the body of any person, including the young person's body and the body of the person encouraging the touching.

Penalty: Hybrid offence –

either a)   summary – maximum penalty is a $2,000 fine or six months in jail, or both

or   b)   indictable – maximum penalty is five years in prison.

Discussion:

- Sexual exploitation is a crime specific to the sexual abuse of young people who are over 14 years of age but have not reached their 18th birthday. The law seeks to protect this age group from sexual exploitation by people who are in a position of trust or authority over them, or by people with whom they have a relationship of dependency. Persons in a position of trust or authority might include parents, teachers, foster parents, coaches, employers, babysitters.

- Where an offence appears to have been committed by a person in a position of trust or authority, child protection workers may be asked by the courts to report on the nature of the young person's relationship with the older person.

Section 159 - **Anal Intercourse**

Element: Acts of anal intercourse are prohibited with children and young people under 18.

Exceptions: Anal intercourse is not a crime if:

- the act takes place in private ("in private" is defined in this section as a place where only two persons are present), and
- both parties consent to the act, and
- both parties are at least 18 years old or are husband and wife.

Penalty: Hybrid offence –

either a)   summary – maximum penalty is a $2,000 fine or six months in jail, or both

or   b)   indictable – maximum penalty is 10 years in prison.

Discussion:

- The new law lowers the age of consent to anal intercourse from 21 to 18 years.

- In any child sexual abuse investigation, any acts of anal intercourse described by the young person or child are illegal, even if other acts described by the young person seem to fall within the provisions that would allow a defence of consent. Young persons under 18 are deemed unable to consent to anal intercourse unless they are husband and wife.

Section 160 - **Bestiality**

Elements: Every person

- who has sexual intercourse or other sexual activity with an animal, or
- who compels someone else to have sexual intercourse or other sexual activity with an animal, or
- who has sexual intercourse or other sexual activity with an animal in the presence of a child under 14, or
- who incites a child under 14 to have sexual intercourse or other sexual activity with an animal.

Penalty: Hybrid offence –

either a)   summary – maximum penalty is a
              $2,000 fine or six months in jail, or
              both

or   b)   indictable – maximum penalty is 10
              years in prison.

Discussion:

- Two new offences relative to children are created in this
  section. It becomes a special offence to commit bestiality
  in the presence of a child under 14 or to incite a child
  under 14 to commit bestiality.

Section 170 - **Parent or Guardian Procuring Sexual Activity of a Child**

Element: Every parent or guardian of a child under 18

- who procures (prevails upon or induces) the
  child to become involved in an illegal sexual
  activity with any person, other than the parent or
  guardian.

Penalty: Indictable –

- if the child is under 14, the maximum
  penalty is five years in prison
- if the child is 14 or more but under 18, the
  maximum penalty is two years in jail.

Discussion:

- This is always deemed to be an indictable offence.

- When interviewing adolescents who may have been victims of this kind of abuse, it may be useful to ask them the earliest age at which they recollect such activity beginning, because this may change the penalty for the offender.

- When interviewing child or adolescent victims of sexual abuse, it should be established whether a parent or guardian encouraged them to engage in sexual activity with other people. Exploration of this issue helps ascertain whether the parents or guardians may have contributed to the exploitation, even though they themselves may not have directly abused the child or young person.

Section 171 - Householder Permitting Sexual Activity

Elements: An owner, manager or someone who assists in the management or control of premises

- who knowingly permits a child under 18 to be in or on the premises
- for the purpose of engaging in an illegal sexual activity (any sexual activity prohibited by the *Criminal Code*).

Penalty: Indictable offence –

- if the child is under 14, the maximum penalty is five years in prison
- if the child is 14 or more but under 18, the maximum penalty is two years in jail.

Discussion:

- The term "premises" would cover many places, including a house, a place of business, a house trailer or even a single room.

- As with the prohibition on parents or guardians against procuring sexual activities, allowing anyone under 18 to use a place to engage in illegal sexual activity is a serious (indictable) offence.

Section 173(2) - **Exposing Genitals to a Child**

Elements: Every person

- in any place
- who exposes his or her genitals to a child under 14
- for a sexual purpose.

Penalty: Summary offence – maximum penalty is a $2,000 fine or six months in jail, or both.

Discussion:

- The type of unwanted sexual act reported most often to the Badgley Committee was indecent exposure, typically a man exposing his genitals to a young girl or a group of girls.

Section 179(1)(b) - **Vagrancy**

Elements: Everyone who has been convicted of sexual assault, one of the sexual touching offences, bestiality or exposure involving a child

- found loitering in or near a playground, school, public park or bathing area.

Penalty: Summary offence – maximum penalty is a $2,000 fine or six months in jail, or both.

Discussion:

- The crime of vagrancy has been committed if all the above elements are proven.

Offences in Relation to Juvenile Prostitution

Section 212(2) - **Living off Avails of Child Prostitution**

Elements: Every person

- who lives wholly or in part off the profits of prostitution
- of a child under 18.

Penalty: Indictable offence – maximum penalty is 14 years in prison.

Discussion:

- Prostitution itself is not against the law in Canada. But it is an offence to:

  – keep or be an inmate of a bawdy house

  – procure or live off the avails of prostitution (pimping)

  – communicate in a public place for the purpose of prostitution

  – obtain or attempt to obtain the sexual services of a juvenile prostitute.

- Under Section 212(3), evidence that a person lives with or is habitually in the company of a prostitute or lives in a common bawdy house is proof, in absence of evidence to the contrary, that the person lives off the avails of the prostitute. This means that once this evidence is presented to the court, it is up to the accused to prove that he or she was not living off the profits of prostitution. This presumption shifts the "burden of proof" from the Crown to the accused.

- The maximum penalty for this offence is 14 years in prison, a higher maximum penalty than that of 10 years in prison for the related offence of attempting to obtain the services of an adult prostitute.

Section 212(4) - **Attempting to Obtain the Sexual Services of a Child**

Elements: Every person

- who obtains, or attempts to obtain for consideration, the sexual services
- of a young person under 18.

Penalty: Indictable offence – maximum penalty is five years in prison.

Discussion:

- The previously existing section, which imposed a time limit for the laying of this charge, has been repealed.

- "Consideration" could include paying for sexual services with cash or drugs, or providing clothes or shelter in exchange for sexual services.

- The new offence recognizes the seriousness of the problem of juvenile prostitution by making it an indictable offence to attempt to obtain or to obtain the sexual services of a child under 18 and by placing responsibility in the hands of the customer of the juvenile prostitute.

- It is not a defence to this crime for the accused to say that he or she believed the young person was over 18. The accused has to prove that all reasonable steps (i.e., asking for identification to determine age) were taken to make sure that the prostitute was at least 18.

- Although it is an offence for an adult to engage the services of a juvenile prostitute, the young person is not committing a crime by being a prostitute. However, he or she may be charged with a related offence. For instance, a young person communicating in a public place for the purpose of prostitution could be charged under the *Criminal Code* but would be tried under the provisions of the *Young Offenders Act*. As well, a child welfare agency may take action to find the young person in "need of protection" through child welfare proceedings.

Previously Existing Offences Still in Force

The new offences have been added to the *Criminal Code* in order to better reflect the nature of child sexual abuse, and so prosecute offenders more effectively. However, it is possible that a person who sexually abuses a child could be charged with one of the previously existing offences related to sexual assault. A brief description of these follows.

Section 155 - **Incest**

Element: Having sexual intercourse with a blood relation.

Penalty: Indictable offence – maximum penalty is 14 years in prison.

Discussion:

- Blood relations include a parent, child, brother, sister, half brother, half sister, grandparent, grandchild.

- No person may be found guilty of this offence if he or she was under restraint, duress or fear at the time of the sexual intercourse. For example, a father and daughter having intercourse could potentially both be charged with incest, but if the daughter was forced in some way she would not be charged.

Section 172 - **Corrupting Children**

Elements: Endangering the morals of children (under age 18) or rendering home an unfit place for the child.

Penalty: Indictable offence – maximum penalty is two years in jail.

Discussion:

- Proceedings under this section can be initiated only with the consent of the provincial or territorial attorney general or at the initiative of a recognized society for the protection of children. This means that the police and the crown prosecutor must ask for permission before they lay charges. A child protection agency, however, does not have to ask for permission from the attorney general before initiating child protection proceedings.

- A previously existing time limit for laying this charge has been repealed as part of the amendments to the *Criminal Code*. A complaint can now be made at any time.

Section 173(1) - **Indecent Acts**

Elements: Performing an indecent act

- in a public place in the presence of one or more persons
- in any place, with intent to insult or offend any person.

Penalty: Summary conviction – maximum penalty is a $2,000 fine or six months in jail, or both.

Discussion:

- This section covers situations where a person indecently exposes himself or herself to someone 14 years of age or over.

- Subsection 173(2) has been added to this provision to deal with exposure of a person's genital organs for a sexual purpose to children under 14 (see page 51).

Section 271 - **Sexual Assault**

Elements: Applying force to another person

- directly or indirectly
- without consent
- under circumstances of a sexual nature.

Penalty: Hybrid offence –

either	a)	summary – maximum penalty is a $2,000 fine or six months in jail, or both
or	b)	indictable – maximum penalty is 10 years in prison.

Discussion:

- In the case of *Regina v. Chase*, the Supreme Court of Canada observed that a sexual assault is an assault that is committed in circumstances of a sexual nature, such that the sexual integrity of a victim is violated. In determining whether or not a sexual assault has taken place, a court may consider relevant the part of the body touched, words and gestures accompanying the act and all other circumstances surrounding the conduct, including the intent, purpose or motive of the accused to the extent that it may appear from the evidence.

- The lack of consent is a key element of this offence. Subsection 271(2), which referred to the defence of consent if the accused is less than three years older than the victim, has been repealed. The defence of consent is now dealt with under Section 150.1. (This is discussed in detail on pages 59 and 60.)

Section 272 - Sexual Assault with a Weapon, Threats to a Third Party or Causing Bodily Harm

Elements: Committing sexual assault while

- carrying, using or threatening to use a weapon or imitation of a weapon, or
- threatening bodily harm to a person other than the victim, or
- causing bodily harm to the victim, or
- being party to this offence with someone else.

Penalty: Indictable – maximum penalty is 14 years in prison.

Discussion:

- When investigating allegations of sexual abuse, interviewers should attempt to determine if threats or weapons were used.

- It may not always be obvious that someone has suffered bodily harm during a sexual assault. Or, time may have passed and the injuries may have healed. An interviewer should ask if the child was physically hurt in any way.

- Threatening to hurt the victim's child is an example of "threats to a third party".

Section 273 - **Aggravated Sexual Assault**

Elements: Wounding, maiming, disfiguring or endangering the life of the victim while committing the sexual assault.

Penalty: Indictable – maximum penalty is life imprisonment.

Discussion:

- Wounding generally means inflicting some kind of cut, laceration or bruise; maiming means causing some kind of crippling injury; disfigurement means causing some visible disfiguring damage to the person.

- This is the most serious of the three sexual assault offences and carries the stiffest penalty.

Defences

The *Criminal Code* not only defines crimes but it also, in some cases, spells out what defences can be considered. For instance, consent is a defence to the charge of sexual assault when two adults are involved. If the court is convinced that there was consent to the sexual activity, no crime has been committed.

Section 150.1, a new amendment to the *Criminal Code*, deals with the defence of consent where the accused is charged with a child sexual abuse crime. An accused person may not justify a sexual act with a young person or child by saying that the victim agreed to what happened.

However, in order not to criminalize normal sexual activity between consenting adolescents who are close in age, the law makes some exceptions to this general principle. If the "victim" is 12 or 13 but under the age of 14, and the accused is 12 or more but under 16 and is less than two years older than the victim, the accused may put forward as a defence that the young person consented to the activity. If these conditions were present and the court believes there was consent, then it will not convict the accused.

With respect to all young people under the age of 18, consent is not a defence if the accused is in a position of trust or authority over the victim or if the victim is dependent on the accused.

For sexual offences that apply to specific age groups, it is not a defence for the accused to say he or she believed that the victim was over the specified age unless the accused took all **reasonable steps** to learn the victim's age. (For example, looking at a proof of age card, driver's licence or birth certificate.)

Questions and Answers

Johnny Smith, age seven, sits on the porch while the police and the child protection worker are inside the house interviewing his five-year-old sister, Susan. Susan says that their new stepfather frequently undresses her, fondles her genitals and makes her touch his penis. Johnny is interviewed next and reluctantly says that sex acts, including anal intercourse, were also performed on him. The children say they complied because their stepfather told them he would "give them the belt" if they did not cooperate.

Q: What charges might be laid?

A: With respect to Susan, the stepfather might be charged with:

- sexual interference
- invitation to sexual touching
- sexual assault
- sexual assault with threat to cause bodily harm to a third party.

With respect to Johnny, the stepfather could be charged with all of the above and also with having anal intercourse with a minor.

Case Example

Jim, a new boarder in the house, frequently invites young boys in the neighbourhood to visit his room to see his comic-book collection. One of the boys finally tells his teenage brother that Jim has been giving the youngsters money for performing fellatio (putting their mouths on his penis). The police are called but Jim claims that he is innocent, saying he "never laid a hand on the kids".

Q : Can Jim be charged, considering that he did not "assault" the children?

A : Under the previous law it might have been difficult to lay charges against Jim, but not under the new law. Jim could be charged under Section 151 (sexual interference), and/or Section 212(4) (attempting to obtain the sexual services of a child for a consideration).

Case Example

Linda, age 13, and her boyfriend, Joe, age 14, are found by Linda's parents engaged in petting (Joe's hands are under Linda's blouse). Linda's parents are angry with her and her father "hits the roof" about her morals. Linda is afraid of her father and claims that Joe forced her into the fondling activity. Linda's parents call the police.

Q : Could Joe be charged with an offence covered under the child sexual abuse law?

A : Perhaps. But if he is charged he may defend himself by saying that his activity was not illegal because:

- he is less than two years older than Linda,
- he is under 16, and
- Linda consented.

Every case has its unique events and circumstances that will determine whether or not a charge should be laid and what the defences to the charge may be.

Q : Is the new child sexual abuse legislation applicable to incidents of sexual abuse that occurred before January 1, 1988?

A : No. Incidents of child sexual abuse that occurred before January 1, 1988, will lead to charges under the legislation that existed prior to the changes. With respect to the changes in the rules of evidence, there is some debate as to whether the courts will apply these new rules of evidence to incidents of child sexual abuse that occurred before January 1, 1988. A crown prosecutor could answer any questions on this point.

Chapter 4

Children
as Witnesses

Changes to the *Criminal Code* Relating to Children's Testimony

As part of the reform of the law on child sexual abuse, substantial changes have been made to lessen the disadvantages experienced by children appearing as witnesses without detracting from the rights of accused persons. A summary of the changes in the rules regarding the testimony of children follows. Changes have been made to both the *Canada Evidence Act* and the *Criminal Code*. Each section is described and is followed by a brief discussion of some of the implications of the new rules.

Please note that the sections of the *Canada Evidence Act* and the *Criminal Code* are paraphrased for simplicity. Readers should refer to the legislation for the exact text of the law.

Section 274 - **Corroboration Not Required**

It is not essential to have additional evidence to corroborate (support) the testimony of a child victim or witness in order to convict someone of a sexual offence. The evidence of the victim or witness may be sufficient to secure a conviction.

Discussion:

- This section acknowledges that child sexual abuse usually takes place in private without any witnesses and that there is usually little physical evidence. It allows for a conviction without requiring further corroborative evidence. However, as in all criminal cases, guilt must be proved beyond a reasonable doubt.

- This rule eliminating the necessity for corroboration was first applied in 1983 to sexual assault cases, and has now been extended to apply to the new laws on child sexual abuse.

- Although corroboration is not required, it is still important to obtain as much evidence as possible.

- This section does not mean that the court **must** convict a person on the evidence of a child alone. It means that the court **may** convict on this alone if it is satisfied beyond a reasonable doubt (on the basis of the child's evidence) that the accused committed the offence and if it decides no further evidence is required in support of this.

Section 275 - **Rules Respecting Recent Complaint Abrogated**

Under the old "recent complaint" rule, if the child victim failed to complain immediately after the offence, this fact could be used to discount the complainant's credibility. This rule was revoked for all sexual assault offences in the 1983 amendments to the *Criminal Code*. The new law also eliminates this rule with respect to child sexual abuse offences.

Discussion:

- It is not necessary for the child victim to have reported the offence to someone soon after the incident; the credibility of the report is not automatically weakened by a delay in reporting.

- Delayed disclosure of sexual abuse has been described as a common pattern. Changing the law on recent complaint acknowledges a new understanding about the reluctance of sexual abuse victims to come forward. Child victims should nevertheless be asked if they can explain the reason for the delay in their disclosure. The answer to this question may reveal possible coercion that may constitute relevant evidence.

Section 276 - **No Evidence Concerning Sexual Activity**

Strict limitations exist on an accused's ability to present evidence of other sexual activity by a victim of sexual assault. These limitations are now extended to all new child sexual abuse offences.

Discussion:

- This section places limits on questions concerning the child victim's previous sexual activities. No questions may be asked about a child victim's prior sexual activity with a person other than the accused except:

  – as a rebuttal to evidence about such sexual activity first presented by the Crown

  – to prove the actual offender is someone else, or

  – where the other sexual activity occurred at the same time as the conduct that has led to the charge before the court and where this evidence relates to the issue of consent.

- If the accused wants to present evidence about previous sexual activity the court will hold a hearing behind closed doors to determine if this line of questioning will be allowed.

- Advance written notice of the intention to ask the court to allow questioning about other sexual activity must be given to the crown prosecutor. This will allow the Crown time to notify the young victim or witness so that he or she can be given help to deal with the emotional impact of this kind of questioning, should the court rule in favour of the defence.

- If the court makes an order allowing defence counsel to examine the child on sexual history, the child may need additional supportive counselling from a specialist.

Section 277 - **Reputation Evidence**

Evidence of the child victim's sexual reputation is not admissible for the purpose of challenging or supporting the victim's credibility.

Discussion:

- Although the sexual behaviour patterns of the child or young person may be highly relevant in therapeutic counselling, this information is not admissible in evidence for the purpose of either challenging or supporting the child or young person's credibility in court.

Section 486(2.1) - **Testimony Outside the Courtroom**

A judge can allow a child victim under the age of 18 to present his or her evidence outside the courtroom or behind a screen or other device within the courtroom so the victim does not have to see the accused when testifying. This procedure is allowed if the judge believes it necessary in order to obtain a full and candid account of the facts of the offence from the child. (As this handbook went to press, screens or closed-circuit television facilities were not available in all court locations.)

Discussion:

- An attempt should be made to determine if the child will be able to give a full and candid account of the events in the presence of the accused. The crown prosecutor should be advised before the trial of any specific fears expressed by the child or if the child's behaviour indicates his or her ability to testify with the accused present may be impaired.

- It should not be assumed that the use of a screen or an out-of-courtroom setting will ensure that the child will not feel anxious or intimidated. The goal of this provision is to allay these feelings to the extent that the child will be able to communicate fully and candidly. Children whose anxiety is so severe that special arrangements are made to hear their evidence will likely remain in need of support. Use of out-of-courtroom arrangements does not replace therapeutic counselling.

- The child may testify outside the courtroom only if arrangements are made so that the accused, the judge, and the jury, if there is one, can watch the testimony via closed-circuit television or by some other means. Also, the accused must be able to communicate with his or her lawyer while the evidence is being presented. It is more likely that the child would remain in the courtroom, with a barrier set up so that the child would not have to see the accused while testifying.

- These courtroom procedures are allowed:

  - only in cases relating to child sexual abuse and sexual assault (under the named sections)

  - only for the victim, not for other child witnesses

  - only if the presiding judge believes it is necessary in order to obtain a full and candid account of the facts of the offence from the child

  - only if the accused is able to hear the testimony and communicate with his or her lawyer at all times.

Section 486(3) and (4) - **Order Restricting Publication**

The child victim, any witness under the age of 18 or the crown prosecutor can ask for an order restricting the publication or broadcast of any information that could disclose the identity of the victim or witness. The judge, at the first reasonable opportunity, must tell any victim or witness under 18 of the right to make such an application.

Discussion:

- Children may be asked by the presiding judge if they wish to make an application to limit the publication or broadcast of any information that would disclose their identities. They should be prepared to answer this question. Ordinarily, prior arrangements should be made with the crown prosecutor by the child, parent or advocate for the child to request a publication ban.

- In cases involving sexual abuse by a parent or relative, the publication or broadcast of the name of the accused may also be prohibited, as this would identify the child victim.

- Once a request has been made, a judge must order a publication ban.

Section 715.1 - **Videotaped Evidence of Complaint**

A videotape of the testimony of a child victim can be used in court, if it was made within a reasonable time after the alleged offence and if the child adopts the contents of the videotape while testifying.

Discussion:

- This applies only to offences of a sexual nature. There is no legislated admissibility of videotapes for other kinds of offences.

- The use of videotaped evidence does not mean that the child does not have to testify in court. At the least, the child must appear in court to confirm the contents of the videotape and may be subject to cross-examination on what he or she says, both on the videotape and on the witness stand.

- When videotaped interviews are conducted, the interviewing technique may be intensively scrutinized for any indication of leading or suggestive questions.

- Each jurisdiction will have to devise a system for dealing with this type of evidence. Videotaping practices should be developed and established in consultation with the police and crown prosecutors.

- Videotaped interviews should take place as soon as possible after the complaint is received.

- Special procedures should be followed when the videotape is made. A clock or time code should be visible in the video shot, and the videotape recorder should be kept running during the full interview. Even if the child leaves the room for a few minutes the tape should continue to record. This is necessary to establish that the tape has not been edited.

- The videotape should start with a statement giving the date, time and place of the interview, name of the child and name(s) of the interviewer(s).

- Documentation should be maintained to indicate why the videotaped interview with the suspected victim was not made closer in time to the alleged incident of sexual abuse.

- Labelling, storage and copying of videotaped interviews of suspected victims of child sexual abuse should be carefully documented and controlled. The crown prosecutor and police should be consulted for appropriate procedures.

Changes to the *Canada Evidence Act* to Deal with Child Witnesses

Section 16 - **Testimony**

The new rules now make it easier for courts to accept the testimony of children, provided that they are able to communicate the evidence. A child's testimony can be heard after the child takes an oath to tell the truth (swearing on the Bible or other religious document such as the Koran) or makes a solemn affirmation (swearing on one's honour to tell the truth). In some cases, a child can give testimony on simply promising to tell the truth.

Discussion:

- The court will automatically ask children under 14 or persons whose mental capacity is challenged whether they understand the meaning of an oath or solemn affirmation. If they understand and are able to communicate the evidence, they can testify after taking an oath or making a solemn affirmation.

- If the person or child does not understand the meaning of an oath or affirmation, but the judge decides the witness is "able to communicate the evidence", the witness may testify by making a promise to tell the truth.

- The definition of "able to communicate the evidence" will be interpreted and determined by the court.

- The evidence of a child testifying, after promising to tell the truth, is as persuasive as other evidence. There is no legal requirement for corroboration. On the other hand, judges may comment on the weight to be given to a child or young person's testimony just as they may with an adult's testimony.

- Preparation of child witnesses should include a discussion of the importance of telling the court about "what really happened" and of telling the truth. It may also focus on helping the child to communicate through words and possibly demonstrations (e.g., using sexually explicit dolls).

- Social workers should document the child's ability to communicate, both verbally and through drawings and demonstrations, and provide this information to the crown prosecutor before court proceedings begin.

- The question of whether a particular child or young person will be able to testify is often a concern, and may influence the decision as to whether to lay a charge. In the past, there has been a bias against bringing very young children forward as witnesses, although in recent years more and more children of very young years (down to age three-and-a-half or four) have given testimony. The language of the legislation appears to be broad enough to allow quite young children to testify as long as they are able to communicate the evidence and to promise to tell the truth. Assessment of the child's developmental maturity, emotional strength or potential to become emotionally stronger may be an important part of the child protection worker's role in advising the police or crown prosecutor about the child's ability to be a credible witness.

Subsection 4(2) -**Spouse of Accused Compellable Witness**

In most criminal cases, the spouse of the accused cannot be required to testify for the prosecution. However, spouses of persons accused of sexual offences may be compelled by the crown prosecutor to give evidence. This includes spouses of persons accused of child sexual abuse offences.

Discussion:

- Therapeutic counselling of non-offending spouses should take this provision into account. A husband or wife of the accused can be subpoenaed and required to testify.

- When a non-offending spouse is a competent and compellable witness for the Crown, conversations between spouses during the marriage that are relevant to the charge against the accused spouse are not privileged and can be brought up in court.

Summary

The changes in the rules of evidence and the rules regarding the testimony of children have been designed to make it easier for children to testify, offsetting the disadvantages they have previously experienced owing to their immaturity, undeveloped communication skills and lack of experience in speaking in public. The issues related to child witnesses are complex and the implementation of these reforms will require a high degree of skill and effort by everyone involved.

Questions
and
Answers

Q : Does the use of a videotape of a child victim's statement mean that the child will not have to appear in court as a witness?

A : No. At a minimum, the child victim will have to appear in court, be accepted by the judge as a witness and then confirm the contents of the videotape (see pages 74 and 75 on the testimony of children). It is possible that the crown prosecutor will also want to ask the child other questions so that evidence in addition to the contents of the tape can be included.

The child may be cross-examined by the defence lawyer on the contents of the videotape and on any other statements made as a witness.

Q : Will the defence have an opportunity to screen the videotape before the trial?

A : Although the answer to this is not entirely clear, it is generally believed that the defence would have the same access to videotapes that it has for written documents. The timing of their release may be in question, although the practice seems to be developing to allow defence early access to these tapes.

Q : Is it possible that the child will never see the accused in court?

A : This is not likely. The process of the child's being accepted as a witness may occur in view of the accused. Whether the child can testify from behind a barrier or in a room outside the courtroom will be decided by the trial judge after hearing arguments about this from the crown prosecutor and defence counsel; the child may be on the witness stand during this process. The child may also be asked to identify the accused as the one who committed the offence. Furthermore, unless special arrangements are made, there is always a possibility that the child will encounter the accused in the corridor or on the way into the courtroom. A child protection worker or victim support worker may want to be present to support the child during such times.

Q : Can a child protection worker testify on behalf of the child, telling the court what he or she was told by the child?

A : No. The accused has a right to hear the evidence against him or her directly from the person who has firsthand knowledge of the facts. One generally cannot testify about what someone else said about a third person.

Chapter 5

Helping
the
Sexually Abused
Child

The Sexually Abused Child

Susan Brown frowned as she surveyed her fifth-grade classroom. She had assigned the class an essay, and most of the children had their heads bent over in concentration as they applied pen to paper. But in a corner seat, curly-haired Ruth was again sagging into a mid-morning nap. This had been developing into an almost daily occurrence over the last couple of months. Sighing, Susan decided to allow the child to doze off. Ruth had changed from a perky, industrious youngster into a sad-faced little girl who had difficulty concentrating on anything.

At the lunch break the teacher gently awakened the child and asked her if something was wrong. Ruth returned her teacher's gaze, burst into tears and said she had to sleep at school because she couldn't sleep at home. If she fell asleep she would wake up to find her mother's new boyfriend "doing things" to her. So, she stayed awake.

Aware that provincial legislation requires professionals to report child abuse, Susan Brown telephoned the local child protection agency saying she was concerned that Ruth was being sexually abused.

This account, based on a real case, is a fairly typical example of how child sexual abuse complaints are initiated. The teacher's phone call triggers a response by the child welfare system. The child protection authorities must in turn contact the police. The two systems may then work together to ensure the child's safety.

The first step in the response is an investigation. Increasingly, child protection agencies and police forces act cooperatively to conduct the initial investigation. The child protection worker needs information to determine whether the child needs protection; the police officer has a responsibility to determine whether a crime has been committed. Both agencies have the interests of the child as their central concern, but act from different perspectives in seeking to protect the child and maintain law and order.

Many jurisdictions now conduct child sexual abuse investigations under directives laid out in "protocols". These are agreements entered into by the police, child protection authorities and provincial justice authorities. They usually describe what procedures must be followed in an investigation. They describe who must take responsibility for each part of the investigation, how communication should flow between the systems, and so on.

For example, in Ruth's case, a protocol might require that the child protection agency notify the police of the teacher's complaint and that the child be interviewed by a team consisting of a police officer and a child protection worker. Although the availability of personnel may affect the timing of the investigation, it is generally a goal to coordinate joint investigative procedures. Many protocols extend beyond the initial investigation. They may include inter-agency procedures for referrals for counselling, case review, preparation of the child to testify at the criminal trial, and post-trial monitoring and review.

How Do the Systems Respond to Help Ruth?

In general, Ruth's case might be handled as follows:

- The child protection worker notes the call and checks to determine if Ruth was already known as a child at risk.

- The child protection worker notifies the local police force.

Depending on the jurisdiction, a decision will be made as to who will conduct the interview(s): the police, a child protection worker, or both.

- The interview with the child takes place. Depending on the dynamics of the family situation, the interview may be held within the home, at the school, at the child protection agency or at the police station. In some parts of the country, local school regulations do not allow interviews to take place at the school unless the parents have been notified. Increasingly, however, investigating authorities and school boards have established agreements that allow interviews to take place within the school. If the abuse involves a parent, and the regulations do not allow interviews to take place within the school, the police or child protection agency will likely decide to interview the child somewhere other than the school.

- In this case, as in all others, the alleged offender should not be alerted to the investigation prior to his or her interview with the police.

- The police initiate their investigation. They may decide to interview the alleged abuser, who may refuse to answer questions – no one is obliged to participate in such an interview.

- If a decision to lay a charge is made, the police may arrest the accused. At that time, the accused is immediately told of his or her right to retain and instruct a lawyer. Once charges are laid, court proceedings as described in Chapter 2 are set in motion.

- The child protection worker and the police officer decide whether Ruth should have an emergency medical examination. If there is no emergency, an examination is conducted as part of a general checkup that should, however, include examination of the genitals and rectal area, and the taking of oral and genital swabs to test for venereal disease. If the parents refuse to consent to an examination, the child protection worker may want to consider if this refusal could mean that the child is "in need of protection". A medical examination may have to be ordered. (For instance, a non-offending mother might refuse to allow a medical examination because she fears it would incriminate her spouse.)

• The child protection worker must also determine if, in his or her opinion, the child can be safely allowed to return home. This usually depends on a number of factors. Does the alleged offender live with the child? If the offender is a parent, does it appear that the non-offending parent or guardian will be supportive? Will the child be pressured to retract his or her statement? The child protection agency will need to determine whether the child's continued safety can be supervised on a voluntary basis, or whether it is necessary to have the child found "in need of protection" by a family court judge. If this is the case, the court may then issue orders for the child protection agency to supervise the child or remove him or her to a safe place such as a foster home or group home.

Because the findings of a child sexual abuse investigation can result in a powerful response that has serious implications both for the child and the alleged offender, the investigation must be conducted with the utmost thoroughness and objectivity. And because the child victim is usually the primary source of information, the initial interview with the child is fundamental in determining subsequent action.

Interviewing Suspected Child Victims

The complexity of conducting a child sexual abuse investigative interview cannot be underestimated. Interviewing skills are developed over time and through ongoing training and practice. In general, these interviews should be conducted by experienced child protection workers and police officers, and several factors should be taken into consideration.

The goal of the interview is to obtain full and comprehensive information as to whether sexual abuse has occurred. In the interview, the child should be treated with dignity, respect and warmth.

The investigator's mind must be open to all possibilities: that sexual abuse occurred, that there was no abuse, or that the child or the person who reported an apparent incident may have misinterpreted the events. As well, they must be aware of the dynamics of abuse and victimization, and the reasons why children sometimes minimize sexual abuse or recant previous accounts of abuse.

Each interview takes on a life of its own; consequently, interview techniques must be adapted and modified to the unique circumstances of each case. Every case should be approached objectively and assessed on its own merits.

some current interview practices

The interview with the child may consist of straightforward questioning, but may also be supplemented by the use of various play objects such as puppets, dolls (both regular and sexually explicit), drawing materials, dollhouses and toy telephones. Reassurance, adaptability, and spontaneity in responding to the child help to create an atmosphere of trust and security, especially if the interview is led in a gentle progression from less sensitive to more sensitive areas. Most interviewers proceed slowly with questioning and do not attempt to rush or pressure the child.

Research is currently under way to develop a standardized format for questioning children in child sexual abuse cases. Generally, interviewing guidelines now in use recommend putting the child at ease, asking questions to ensure that the child knows the difference between telling the truth and lying, and then proceeding through a series of **non-leading questions** to encourage the child to relate what, if anything, occurred. The interview attempts to clarify details and obtain comprehensive information; it is not designed to confirm a presupposed presence of abuse, but rather to discover if abuse has occurred and if so, to determine its nature and extent.

Experience has shown that although some children are able to discuss their experiences quite freely, others are very anxious during investigative interviews. Noting behavioural indicators of anxiety may help the interviewer realize when the discussion is approaching areas that might reveal information about an abusive incident.

Some investigators have found that play objects help children relax and become more communicative. It is believed that a child who consistently gives the same account through a variety of play materials is more likely to be relating an event that actually happened. The use of various playthings may also add clarity to an account. For example, very young children might find it hard to describe "upstairs", but may be able to do this easily if they are using a dollhouse.

Some interviewers draw with the child. For example, they might draw a neutral "gingerbread person" outline of a human figure and invite the child to fill in the eyes, nose and other body parts.

Puppets of animals or of familiar, comfortable figures are sometimes used to help children relax and begin to articulate. The interviewer may use a puppet that talks to another puppet held by the child. Some younger children in particular seem to be more comfortable in speaking, at least initially, through the medium of a puppet. Similarly, some children seem more willing to conduct the interview over a set of toy telephones or by demonstrating with dollhouse figures.

Concern has been raised that anatomically explicit dolls may be inherently suggestive of sexual behaviour. If employed to facilitate an interview, they therefore should be used very carefully. A selection of adult male and female dolls and child male and female dolls should be available. The dolls must be fully clothed at the outset of the interview. The child, not the interviewer, should approach and select the dolls. If the child demonstrates sexually explicit behaviour with the dolls, this may cast light on the information the child has been giving verbally. Sometimes, the interviewer may ask the child to explain verbally what is being demonstrated and ask very specifically if it is intended to represent a real situation.

Research on the use of anatomically explicit dolls and their effectiveness as a diagnostic tool is currently under way.

Where possible, children should be interviewed alone. However, very young or frightened children may need the presence of a parent or other support person. If so, the adult is usually asked to sit behind the child, where the child cannot observe facial reactions. They are also asked not to interfere in the interview or prompt the child.

Other Considerations

videotaping interviews

Videotaping children's interviews serves several purposes. It can help eliminate the trauma caused by repeated interviewing of child victims by the various professionals who become involved; it can serve clinical purposes by enabling experts to assess some of the psychodynamics of sexual abuse, as revealed by the child's behaviour and expressions; and, as discussed in Chapter 4, it can now serve as evidence in criminal court cases. However, children should not be videotaped if there is any indication that the experience would be traumatizing for them.

Because of their potential use in court, videotaped interviews should be conducted by experienced, skilled interviewers who are aware of the legal requirements for making videotapes that might be used as evidence in court. Any videotape made at an early stage should always be carefully labelled and stored. In some parts of the country, specific policies have been developed on making such videotapes.

interviewing adolescents

It is particularly important to give teenagers the time and opportunity to provide as much detail as possible about incidents – not only the sexual acts but also about the clothes that were worn, the time of day, the place, the physical characteristics of the alleged offender.

There may be special problems in investigating sexual abuse offences with teenage victims. They are easily embarrassed. They often appear older than their age. Unlike young children, it cannot be assumed that they lack sexual knowledge. If the abuse has lasted many years, the adolescent may be experiencing serious, entrenched trauma. The young person may have been conditioned by the adult to believe that he or she is responsible for the abuse or was at least an equal participant.

Guilt, confusion and shame may make it very difficult for adolescents to discuss their experiences. Detailed, thoughtful interviewing may be needed over several sessions to provide ample opportunity for full disclosure. In addition, concerns about a false complaint by an adolescent can be laid to rest (or confirmed) by a comprehensive investigation that elicits substantial evidence.

custody and access disputes

The investigation of child sexual abuse cases can be especially sensitive if the child is very young, if a parent is the alleged abuser, and if the primary source of information about the abuse is the other parent. The situation is even more difficult if the alleged abuse has become an issue in a custody dispute. Careful and detailed interviewing of the child and interviews with both parents should be undertaken.

Following the initial investigation to document the allegations and to obtain a comprehensive statement from the child, a more detailed assessment sometimes takes place. This may include separate interviews with the parent or other adults (such as grandparents) who have made the allegations, and a detailed assessment of the child to obtain further clarification of the child's experience.

Some clinicians feel that observation of parent-child interaction may shed light on whether there has been an abusive relationship. Other clinicians take the view that such interviews yield only limited information. It is generally agreed that joint parent-child sessions should never occur if there are strenuous objections from the child or if the child expresses severe anxiety when talking about the parent.

It is **always** necessary to ensure that any contact between an allegedly abusive parent and the child does not occur in violation of a bail order prohibiting contact. Although bail orders can be changed on application to the court by either the crown prosecutor or the defence lawyer, consideration should be given to the effect that such contact might have: for instance, fear or intimidation causing the child to eventually recant the allegations. Generally, such sessions are for behavioural observation only – discussion of the alleged offence is ruled out. This is fundamentally different from therapy sessions, in which the ultimate goal is to have the admitted offender apologize to the child and assume responsibility for the sexual offence.

In cases involving a custody or access dispute, evidence of the alleged abuse may also be presented before a superior court for proceedings under the *Divorce Act*, or before a provincial or territorial youth or family court under provincial statutes related to family law.

allegations against community figures

Investigating allegations against persons in positions of trust or others highly respected in the community is often fraught with difficulty, because investigators, acquaintances and the public generally, have a natural reluctance to believe that such a person could be capable of sexually abusing a child. Objectivity may be difficult to maintain. It is particularly important in such cases to maintain a neutral and thorough approach and to ensure good consultation and coordination between the various systems involved.

multiple victims

Sometimes the same offender has abused a number of young victims over a period of time. Investigating these cases can become quite complex, as a complaint against one person can bring to light other cases of sexual abuse. A further complication can be that the young victims may know each other

– a child protection worker may face problems of confidentiality and other treatment issues. Good liaison with the police, the school, and groups such as the Block Parents Association may be important in these cases.

multiple offenders

There are cases in which a group of abusers exploits a child or group of children. There may be ritualistic elements in such abuse, and the activities could include organized child pornography and child prostitution. Although these occurrences may be rare, they are of particular concern because they often involve very young children and a greater severity of victimization through intimidation, physical injury, drugs or other forms of abuse.

A child protection worker faced with this type of case may find it hard to believe that such events could have occurred. The challenge of overcoming personal revulsion and conducting an investigation according to accepted practice is compounded by the need to act quickly. Media attention can make an investigation even more difficult. Support from superiors and other agencies is essential.

Following the Investigation and Leading Up to the Trial

If a charge is laid following the investigation, the court procedures described in Chapter 2 will be followed. Simultaneously, decisions regarding the welfare of the child will be made.

Close communication between the child protection workers, police and the crown prosecutor is essential during this period, because actions in one system can profoundly affect decision-making in the other. For example, in a case of intrafamilial sexual abuse where an alleged offender is released on condition that he or she have no access to the child, it may be agreed that there is no need to remove the child from the home. However, should the accused be granted a variance of the conditions of release that would allow him or her to return home, the child protection authorities should be aware of this so that they can determine if the child should be removed from the home.

Similarly, the crown prosecutor should be informed of changes in the child protection arrangements that might affect the criminal case. For example, the child protection agency may decide, as an emergency measure, to take the child from the home immediately following its investigation. If the family court later decides to return the child to the home, the crown prosecutor might want to ask the criminal courts to change the accused's condition of release to prohibit contact with the child until the trial is held. A condition can also be set requiring the accused to report to the investigating police agency when the family court returns the child home.

From the earliest stages in a case of child sexual abuse – from the time of a complaint through the investigation and up to, during and after the trial – a continuous flow of information is needed between the systems.

Questions and Answers

Q : Is it up to the child protection worker to investigate a case and determine whether there is cause for laying criminal charges?

A : No. These are police functions. If a child protection worker is the first professional to learn of a possible case of child sexual abuse, the police should be notified immediately. It is not up to this person to screen the case for police.

Q : Must all interviews with children in sexual abuse investigations now be videotaped?

A : No. The legislation permits, but does not require, videotapes to be made. Each agency should develop its own policy on the making and use of videotapes in close consultation with police and crown prosecutors.

Q : Is there any set definition of what constitutes asking a child a "leading" question?

A : No. Whether a child has been unfairly led into making statements can be determined only by the circumstances of each case. Interviewers must consider the context and frame their questions in a way that helps the child feel free to talk, and does not **suggest** an answer to the child. The following standard, developed by Corporal Hunter McDonald of the Royal Canadian Mounted Police (Victoria, B.C.), may be of assistance.

- Open-ended question: "Then what?"

- Focused question: "Was it daylight or dark or are you not sure?"

- Leading question: "Your Mom told me it was at night, isn't that right?"

Ultimately, it will be up to the court to decide what evidence will be admissible at the trial.

Q : If a child protection worker is interviewing a person who begins to confess about having sexually abused a child, what should the child protection worker do?

A : A confession by an abuser about an incident of child sexual abuse must be reported to the police by the child protection worker. Careful notes should be taken about what has been said.

However, a child protection worker has special authority under child protection laws to protect children. This statutory role puts a child protection worker in a particular relationship to people being interviewed. It appears possible that the presence of the worker at such a confession could be argued to have had a coercive effect. Confessions that are coerced or made under duress are deemed to be inadmissible in criminal proceedings.

In presenting the case against the accused, the crown prosecutor would usually want to bring up the confession in court. If the child protection worker's presence during the confession rendered the statement inadmissible, a significant part of the Crown's case could be lost. For these reasons, in many jurisdictions the practice is for child protection workers to **not** be present during police interviews of accused persons.

Chapter 6

The Child Protection Worker and the Sexually Abused Child

The Traditional Role of the Child Protection Worker

The child protection worker traditionally has addressed the problem of child sexual abuse

- through investigation and identification of children in need of protection;

- through case management that ensures the safety of the child by means of supervision and treatment, or by taking the child into custody and placing him or her in a "place of safety" such as a foster home; and

- through prevention of abuse through public education.

New Roles: Greater Involvement in the Criminal Justice Process

Today, new roles are evolving for child protection workers in the fight against child sexual abuse. Many are professional social workers. Functioning in the social service, justice and educational systems – as family counsellors, as victim advocates and as mental health therapists – many are finding new ways to help sexually abused children and their families.

Child protection workers who have knowledge of a particular case may be called to testify about what they have observed or to justify statements they have made in their records. They may be cross-examined by defence counsel, who may challenge their methods of interviewing or data collection to reveal any bias or unfairness.

Recognizing the need to define roles clearly and to ensure appropriate support for children, a number of Canadian jurisdictions have established formalized agreements that set standards of investigative procedure between agencies with mandates to protect children and agencies of the criminal justice system.

pre-trial counselling

Supportive counselling of children who will be appearing as witnesses may also become an expanded role for child protection workers. In pre-trial preparation of child victims, they may offer support and assistance to help reduce the children's anxiety about appearing in court or seeing the accused.

Part of the ongoing work with such children may include therapeutic counselling to counteract feelings of shame or guilt concerning the sexual abuse. Unless they are helped to address and resolve such emotional conflicts, they may find it very difficult to describe their experiences in court.

Pre-trial counselling may also yield information about a child's communication skills and level of understanding, and any specific fears about the trial or the accused. A summary of this information should be given to the crown prosecutor. The child protection worker may also consider accompanying the child at initial meetings with the crown prosecutor in order to establish a bridge of trust between the two.

In consultation with the crown prosecutor, trial proceedings should be explained as simply as possible to child witnesses. They should be made aware of the right to request a ban on publication of their identities, and the possibility of giving evidence behind a screen or in an out-of-courtroom setting if these procedures are available. For younger children, this information should be given to parents or guardians.

The possible introduction in court of a videotaped interview in which abuse was disclosed should also be discussed with the child. In consultation with the crown prosecutor, it may be decided to allow the child to see the videotape before the trial, so that he or she will be better prepared when viewing it in the courtroom and being asked to adopt its contents.

In trial preparation, some practitioners use role-playing, sometimes with puppets, to give children an opportunity to take on the roles of all the different persons who will be in court – not only themselves as witnesses, but also defence counsel, crown prosecutor, judge and defendant. (It is preferable not to role-play the actual case, because this may indicate "coaching" of the child.) As the child imaginatively takes on these roles, anxiety often becomes diffused, questions can be anticipated, and the process and purpose of the trial become clearer as they are examined from new perspectives. Pre-trial visits to an empty courtroom where the child is allowed to explore the setting may have a similar effect of reducing anxiety about a new experience.

As well, it is important to explain to any child the possibility that the accused could be acquitted. It can be hard for a child to understand that, because of the principles of justice (innocent until proven guilty, proof beyond a reasonable doubt, etc.), the court could render a decision that may confuse the child. It might be helpful to describe the presentation of evidence at a trial as pieces of a puzzle – if not enough pieces can be found, the judge (or jury) cannot convict the accused.

A child protection worker should be sensitive to a child's reaction to a "not guilty" verdict. Feelings of self-blame or self-doubt may arise, and additional support for the child may be necessary.

support during trial

On the days the child attends court, the child protection worker can provide support by keeping the child company while waiting, protecting the child from encounters with the accused or persons supporting the accused, and allaying the anxiety of parents or guardians. Providing food, puzzles or books, and paying attention to the child's need to nap or go to the bathroom can also help prevent the escalation of anxiety.

If the child protection worker is also a witness at the trial, he or she may not be allowed in the courtroom except to give evidence. In some courts, witness support workers and victim support workers can provide assistance to children and young persons testifying in criminal cases.

ongoing treatment

As part of counselling families and children where sexual abuse has occurred, more child protection workers are beginning to provide ongoing treatment services; individual, group and family therapy are increasingly being offered to child victims and their families.

Also, as treatment plans for abusers are developed, they may be communicated to both the crown prosecutor and the defence lawyer, with a view to having orders for treatment included in the accused's sentence.

Looking Ahead

The Review Process

The January 1988 amendments to the *Criminal Code* and the *Canada Evidence Act* concerning child sexual abuse signal an intent to provide greater protection to children. No major change such as this can occur, however, without a significant period of learning through experience. As cases move forward under the new rules, the extent to which children are being better protected, and whether this is being achieved without compromising the rights of accused persons, will become increasingly clear.

For this reason, the legislation calls for a parliamentary review to be completed as soon as possible after January 1992. In the spirit of this legislation, the federal Department of Justice is already conducting continuing research as part of an ongoing review process.

Public Education and Professional Development

As the new legal procedures fall into place, there will also be an increased need for public education and professional training and skills development.

Public education to prevent child sexual abuse will remain a vital part of social work practice. Child protection workers are in a unique position to understand the effects of sexual abuse, including the difficulties a child has in disclosing abuse, the effects of disclosure on the child and the family, and the impact on the child of intervention by the social welfare and criminal justice systems. This "insider's view" must be communicated both to the public and to other professionals.

At the same time, professional education is essential: child protection workers need to understand the complexities of the law, while legal professionals require information to better understand both the needs of children and the problems of abusers. Skills development will improve investigative techniques and lead to more effective case management and better inter-system communication and collaboration.

The years ahead will be challenging for professionals and other individuals working with the victims of child sexual abuse. Everyone has an important role to play in this vital task.

GLOSSARY

Accused – A person who is charged with a crime.

Admissible Evidence – Evidence that is relevant to the trial and that can be presented to the court. In some situations, the judge can rule that certain evidence is not admissible and should not be heard.

Affirmation – A legally binding promise to tell the truth. A person who does not want to swear to tell the truth on the Bible or other religious document makes a solemn affirmation to tell the truth.

Arrest – To deprive a person of liberty by legal authority and hold that person in custody.

Bail – Money or property deposited with the court as a guarantee that the accused will come back for a hearing or trial.

Beyond a Reasonable Doubt – The level of proof needed to find a person guilty of having committed a crime.

Canadian Charter of Rights and Freedoms – Part of Canada's Constitution that guarantees certain rights and freedoms.

Charge – A formal accusation that a person has committed a specific crime.

Civil Proceedings – Proceedings related to a court action between private individuals. One individual or company sues another to enforce a private right or redress a private wrong. Civil proceedings are very different from the proceedings at a criminal trial and take place in different courts.

Compellable Witness – A witness who can be forced by subpoena to give evidence in court.

Complainant – A person who states that a crime has been committed.

Confession – A statement made by the accused admitting guilt. If a confession has been made freely and voluntarily, it may be allowed in court as evidence.

Contempt of Court – Interfering with the administration of justice or ignoring the rules of the court.

Corroborating Evidence – Evidence by another witness or source that confirms or supports evidence already given to the court.

Criminal Code – A federal law that sets out most criminal offences in Canada. Some criminal offences are described in other federal laws.

Crown Prosecutor – The lawyer representing the Crown (i.e. the State). At the trial, the crown prosecutor presents evidence of the crime and tries to prove that the accused committed the crime. This person may also be referred to as the crown attorney, crown counsel, or simply, the Crown.

Defence Counsel – The lawyer representing the defendant, the accused person.

Defendant – A person who is sued or against whom a legal proceeding has been taken.

Hearsay Evidence – Evidence offered by a witness about things that were not personally observed or experienced **firsthand** but rather were received from another person. Usually, this evidence is not admissible.

Hybrid Offence – A criminal offence that can be prosecuted either by summary conviction or by indictment. The decision as to which way to proceed is made by the crown prosecutor and is based on the seriousness of the offence. A hybrid offence is referred to and may also be known as a dual procedure offence or a mixed offence.

Indictable Offence – The *Criminal Code* divides offences into two categories: indictable and summary conviction offences. An indictable offence is the more serious criminal offence. The punishment for indictable offences can be from two years in jail to life imprisonment (see also "summary conviction offence").

Justice of the Peace – An officer of the court who has some powers of a judge.

No-contact Order – A court order preventing the accused from seeing or speaking to someone.

Oath – A legally binding promise to tell the truth, made by swearing on the Bible or other religious document such as the Koran. A person who does not want to swear on a religious document makes an "affirmation". An affirmation is also a legally binding promise to tell the truth.

Offence – A crime.

Plea – The answer given by an accused when charged with a criminal offence: "guilty" or "not guilty".

Position of Trust or Authority – The child sexual abuse crimes include the concept of a person "in a position of trust or authority". These words are not defined in the *Criminal Code* and so their exact meaning will be determined by the courts. Although the definition will evolve through case law, parents, teachers, coaches and babysitters may be considered to be in a "position of trust or authority" because they have a special relationship to children.

Preliminary Inquiry – A hearing to determine whether there is sufficient evidence against an accused for a criminal case to proceed to trial.

Pre-sentence Report – A description of the accused's family life and personal situation, prepared by a probation officer, which the judge considers when deciding an appropriate sentence.

Probation – A punishment given to a person convicted of an offence, which requires the person to obey certain conditions but does not require him or her to pay a fine or spend time in jail.

Recent Complaint – The rule requiring the court to hold in doubt the testimony of a sexual abuse victim who did not complain to someone immediately after the offence occurred has been abrogated. Consequently, the credibility of a victim's disclosure of an offence is not weakened by a delay in reporting – it is now not necessary for a child victim to have reported an offence to someone soon after the incident.

Relationship of Dependency – The child sexual abuse crimes include the concept of a "relationship of dependency". These words are not defined in the *Criminal Code* and so their exact meaning will be determined by the courts. Although the definition will evolve through case law, a relationship of dependency may be considered to be one in which a child or young person relies on someone else for financial support and shelter (see also "position of trust or authority").

Sentencing Hearing – A hearing held after the accused has been found guilty of a crime. The judge can hear evidence to help in deciding on an appropriate punishment.

Sexual Purpose – The crimes of sexual interference, invitation to sexual touching, and sexual exploitation all include the phrase "sexual purpose". These words are not defined in the *Criminal Code* and so their exact meaning will be determined by the courts. A sexual purpose might be the sexual arousal or gratification of the person who initiates the activity.

Standard of Proof – The minimal level of proof required to find a person guilty in a criminal trial or to reach a finding that the plaintiff's claim is justified in a civil trial. The standard of proof is higher in a criminal trial. To find an accused guilty in a criminal trial, the judge or jury must be convinced "beyond a reasonable doubt" that the accused is guilty. If there is a reasonable possibility that the accused is innocent then he or she must be found not guilty. In a civil trial, proof must be made on the balance of probabilities. The court must find that it is more likely than not that something happened. This is a lower standard of proof than proof "beyond a reasonable doubt".

Subpoena – An order of the court telling a person when and where he or she must appear as a witness.

Summary Conviction Offence – A criminal offence less serious than an indictable offence, with a possible maximum punishment of six months in jail and/or a $2,000 fine (see "indictable offence").

Victim Impact Statement – A statement describing, in writing, the harm done to the victim or the loss suffered by the victim as a result of the crime. A victim impact statement may be considered by the court when deciding on the sentence.

Warrant for Arrest – An order of a justice of the peace or judge, giving the police permission to arrest someone.

Young Person – The *Criminal Code* section on sexual exploitation defines a young person as a person fourteen years of age or more but under the age of eighteen years.

SELECTED READING

Following are selected readings in various aspects of child sexual abuse.

Historical Perspectives and Research

Brown, Angela, and David Finklehor. "Impact of Child Sexual Abuse: A Review of the Research". Family Violence Research Program, Family Research Laboratory, University of New Hampshire. *Psychological Bulletin*, Vol. 99, No. 1, January 1986, American Psychological Association. (Disponible en français sous le titre "Impact de l'exploitation sexuelle de l'enfant : examen de recherche".)

Burgess, Ann W., and M.L. Clark. *Child Pornography and Sex Rings*. Boston: D.C. Heath and Company Limited, 1984.

Butler, Sandra. *Conspiracy of Silence*. San Francisco: Volcano Press, 1978.

Canada. Department of Justice. *Sexual Offences Against Children –* Report of the Committee on Sexual Offences Against Children and Youth. Ottawa: Government of Canada, 1984. (Disponible en français sous le titre *Infractions sexuelles à l'égard des enfants*.)

Carrière, Richard. *Enfance maltraitée et négligée, Un répertoire des ressources communautaires.* Sudbury: Laurentian University, 1984.

Finklehor, David. *Child Sexual Abuse – New Theory and Research*. New York: The Free Press, McMillan, Inc., 1984.

Finklehor, David. *A Sourcebook on Child Sexual Abuse.* Beverly Hills: Sage Publications, 1986.

Goranson, S.E., *Young child interview responses to anatomically correct dolls: Implications for practice and research in child sexual abuse* (unpublished master's thesis). Vancouver: University of British Columbia, 1986.

Herman, Judith. *Father-Daughter Incest.* Cambridge: Harvard University Press, 1981.

King, Mary Ann, and John Yuille. "The Child as a Witness". *Canadian Psychological Association Highlights*, January, 8 (1), 25-27, 1986.

Marron, Kevin. *Ritual Abuse.* Toronto: McLelland-Bantam, Inc., 1988.

Russell, Diana E.H. *Sexual Exploitation and Workplace Harassment.* Beverly Hills M.S.A.: Sage Publications, 1984.

Schlesinger, Benjamin. *Sexual Abuse of Children in the 1980s.* Toronto: University of Toronto Press, 1986.

Zeller, Christine, and Camille Messier. *Des enfants maltraités au Québec.* Quebec: Les Publications du Québec, 1987.

Investigation and Assessment

de Young, Mary. "A Conceptual Model for Judging the Truthfulness of a Young Child's Allegations of Sexual Abuse". *Journal of the American Orthopsychiatric Association*, October 1986.

Halliday, L. *Sexual Abuse: Interviewing Techniques for Police and other Professionals.* Campbell River, B.C.: Ptarmigan Press, 1986.

Jaffe, P., and S.K. Wilson. *Court Testimony of Child Sexual Abuse Victims: Emerging Issues in Clinical Assessments.* London, Ontario: London Family Court Clinic, 1986.

Quebec. Ministère de la Santé et des services sociaux. *Protocole d'évaluation et d'intervention médico-sociale.* Bibliothèque nationale du Québec, Gouvernement du Québec, 1988.

Service aux familles et à l'enfance pour la région Nipissing. *Lignes directrices et procédures pour la prévention coordonnée de l'abus des enfants dans le district de Nipissing.* Nipissing, Ontario, 1985.

Wells, Mary. *Guidelines for Investigative Interviewing of Child Victims of Sexual Abuse.* The Metropolitan Chairman's Special Committee on Child Abuse. Ottawa: National Clearinghouse on Family Violence, Health and Welfare Canada, 1983. (Disponible en français sous le titre *Lignes directrices pour l'entrevue exploratoire avec l'enfant victime d'agression sexuelle.*)

Yuille, J.C. "The Systematic Assessment of Children's Testimony". *Canadian Psychology*, 1988, 29.3.

Treatment

Crivillé, Albert. *Parents maltraitants, enfants meurtris.* Paris: Editions ESF, 1987.

Fortune, Marie M. *Sexual Violence, The Unmentionable Sin.* (For pastoral counsellors.) New York: The Pilgrim Press, 1983.

Giard, Marie. "Place et rôle de l'entraide dans le traitement de l'agression sexuelle". *Le travailleur social*, Winter, 1988.

MacFarlane, Kee, et al. *Sexual Abuse of Young Children.* New York: The Guilford Press, 1986.

Masson, Jeffrey M. *Assault on Truth.* Penguin Books, 1985.

Miller, Alice. *Thou Shalt Not Be Aware.* Scarborough, Ontario: Meridian Books, The New American Library, 1986.

Porter, Ruth. *Child Sexual Abuse Within the Family.* London: Tavistock Publications Ltd., 1984.

Quebec. *La santé mentale des enfants et des adolescents, vers une approche plus globale.* Bibliothèque nationale du Québec, Gouvernement du Québec, 1985.

Sgroi, Suzanne, MD. *Handbook of Clinical Intervention in Child Sexual Abuse.* Lexington: Lexington Books, D.C. Heath and Company, 1982.

Summit, Roland, MD. "The Child Sexual Abuse Accommodation Syndrome". *Child Abuse and Neglect*, Vol. 7, pages 177-193, 1983.

The Perspective of Survivors

Gil, Eliana. *Outgrowing the Pain.* Walnut Creek, California: Launch Press, 1983.

Halliday, Linda. *The Silent Scream.* Toronto: University of Toronto Guidance Centre, 1985.

Ward, Elizabeth. *Father, Daughter Rape.* London: The Women's Press, 1984.

Publications for Children

Canada. Department of Justice. *The Secret of the Silver Horse.* Ottawa: Supply and Services Canada, 1989. (Disponible en français sous le titre *Le secret du petit cheval.*)

Gervais, Jean. *L'étrange voisin de Dominique.* Montréal: Les Éditions Boréal, 1988.

INDEX